UNBROKEN

A Story of Resilience

— *Second Memoir* —

Husam Yaghi

UNBROKEN

ISBN: 979-8-950300-10-3
Published by Yaghi.net
First edition, 2026

Illustrations produced with AI-assisted tools under author direction.

Author's Note

In Beyond Success told you what I built. This book tells you what it cost. It is not a sequel in which the protagonist heals; I am sixty-five and I still wake before dawn. What I can offer is the truth as I currently understand it, which will keep changing.

◈ ◈ ◈

Some of my family members appear in these pages only where their presence is essential to understanding what shaped me, or what is now reshaping me. They are not the subject of this book. Their inner lives, their struggles, and their stories belong to them. Where I have written about them, I have done so with care for their privacy. Where I have stayed silent, I have done so on purpose.

— Husam Yaghi

◈ ◈ ◈

Introduction: The Cost of the Smile

Three days after an award ceremony in Dubai, my daughter asked me a question I couldn't answer.

"Dad, if you're so successful, why do you always look like your mind is somewhere else?"

She was sixteen. The award was real, one of the biggest in my career. The cameras had been bright. Strangers had lined up to shake my hand. I had smiled wide, the kind of smile that ends up in press photos and corporate websites. And the night before the ceremony, I had stared at the hotel ceiling for hours, my chest tight with anxiety I had no current explanation for.

I started giving Tamara my usual answer, about challenges, about staying sharp, the version I had refined over years of polite questions from polite people. The words stopped in my throat. She wasn't a polite stranger. She was my daughter. She had inherited my drive but not my damage, my values but not my scars, and she deserved better than the talking points.

The truth was that I didn't know.

I didn't know why success felt like something that could be taken away at any moment. I didn't know why every triumph arrived with the sharp edge of an old wound. I didn't know why my heart raced before dawn from threats that had ended forty years ago in a country I no longer lived in.

My nephew Jim had died a few months earlier. Forty-one years old, gifted, kind, accomplished, loved by everyone. He had done what we are told to do. He had worked, sacrificed, achieved. None of it had saved him. Standing at his funeral, watching his small son try to understand the unanswerable, I felt the weight of every story I had quietly edited out of my own, every terror I had repackaged as inspiration, every wound I had translated into an inspirational keynote.

I had written *Beyond Success* to show that education and stubbornness could move a refugee child from Amman to American patents. That was true. It was just nowhere near the whole story.

This book is the rest of it.

Tamara's question opened a door I had walked past for thirty years. Behind it was the version of my life I had never written down, because writing it down would mean admitting that the awards hadn't fixed me, the achievements hadn't paid the debt, and the smile in the photographs was real but it was also work.

I am still debugging the model I run on. There's a line from *Mind Bending* that stayed with me: AI learns from patterns. So do humans. We build internal algorithms, childhood, culture, war, success, failure, and they quietly run the show. Two people walk through the same fire and come out with different burns, not because the fire played favorites, but because they were running on different training data.

I am still walking. The boy who walked ten kilometers to school is still walking; he just owns the shoes now. What this book is for is anyone else who is also still walking, who is also carrying something heavy under a respectable suit, who has also wondered why the applause never quite reaches the place where the question lives.

You don't have to be healed to be useful. You don't have to be finished to be worth listening to. That, I think, is what I would have said to my daughter that night if I had been able to find the words. I am finding them now.

❖ ❖ ❖

PART ONE: WHAT THE BODY REMEMBERS

❖ ❖ ❖

Chapter 1

The body keeps score

The wars ended in the 1970s. My nervous system never received the memo.

The bullets, the tank, the staircase are in Beyond Success. What stayed isn't.

I am sixty-five. I sleep badly. I have sleep apnea, the throat that learned to be silent during danger never quite stopped practicing. My body still holds its breath at night the way it held its breath in 1972. I wake before dawn whether or not I want to, my pulse running ahead of my reasons. I can give you the location of every exit in any room I enter within thirty seconds of arrival. I cannot tell you where I left my reading glasses five minutes ago.

This is not discipline. I used to think it was. My mother's steady hands at the saj while bullets cracked over the courtyard became, for me, the template of how a person handles pressure: don't flinch, don't stop the work, finish the bread. I built a forty-year career on that template. It is genuinely useful in a crisis. It is genuinely terrible at letting you rest.

The hypervigilance that kept me alive doesn't know how to retire. Other people tell me to relax and I look at them like they have suggested I learn to breathe underwater. Relaxation is something I observe in others, the way you observe a foreign custom on a holiday, interesting, picturesque, not for me.

There is a phrase psychologists use for this: trauma-informed wisdom. It is supposed to be a compliment. What it really means is that you see things other people don't see, which is valuable in the boardroom and exhausting everywhere else. You prepare for disasters that never arrive. The disaster never arriving doesn't reduce your readiness; it just means tonight wasn't the night. Tomorrow is still the night. Tomorrow is always still the night.

I notice the cost of this most when I am with my daughter. Tamara doesn't have my reflexes. She has never had to know where the exits are. She walks into a room and her shoulders don't move. The first time I caught myself watching her do that, watching her be completely present without scanning for threats, I cried in the car afterward and could not tell my wife why.

What you inherit from war is not opinions about war. It is a setting in your nervous system. Mine is set to *something is about to happen.* It has been set there since I was seven. There is no software update for this. There is only learning to live with it, learning that it has helped me as much as it has hurt me, and learning, slowly, to let small flickers of peace exist without immediately interrogating them.

My mother died believing her steadiness had given me a gift. It had. She never knew it had also given me a sentence. I don't blame her. She was making bread under live fire and we were going to eat. There was no other available choice.

I am writing this on a Tuesday morning in Riyadh at 4:47 a.m. The city is quiet. I have been awake since 4:12. Nothing is wrong. Nothing has been wrong for years.

The body keeps score anyway.

❖ ❖ ❖

Chapter 2

The weight of an inheritance

My father called me *al-mohandes*, the engineer, before I could spell the word. I described that prophecy in *Beyond Success* and made it sound like a gift. It was a gift. It was also a contract I never signed.

The thing about a parent's dream landing in a five-year-old's lap is that the five-year-old can't tell whose dream it is. By the time you are old enough to ask the question, the answer is no longer available to you, because you have already become the answer.

My father had wanted me to be an engineer. 1948 redirected him. The same displacement that took my grandparents' orange groves took his vocational future. So he aimed it at his son, with the fierce, slightly desperate precision of someone who has watched one life end and is trying very hard to start another one through a child. I loved him. I wanted him to be proud. I also genuinely loved engineering, that is the part that makes this complicated. I wasn't dragged into a career I hated. I was placed in a career I was good at and grew to love, and then I spent four decades unable to tell which of those things had come first.

This is the part *Beyond Success* didn't say: every patent I have ever earned has felt partly like mine and partly like a payment. I would stand on stages and watch other engineers accept their awards as personal accomplishments, and I would notice that my own version of the same moment carried a tax. There was always a small voice asking whether this was the right kind of success, whether I had honored the correct sacrifice, whether the work justified what had been spent to make it possible.

Then there was the lawnmower.

I had the machine, I lost focus, his fingers were where they should not have been. I have written this sentence many times. It does not get easier. He never recovered the use of his hands the way they had been before. My father, the man who had built our house in Amman from rocks and mud, who had taught me to use tools, who had earned his living fixing heavy machinery, lost the part of his body he most needed to be the man he was.

He forgave me immediately. *Habibi, accidents happen. This is not your fault.*

I have spent over forty decades trying to disagree with that sentence.

Anger would have been easier. Anger creates clean transactions: the wronged party, the wrongdoer, the punishment, the resolution. His grace gave me nowhere to put the weight. So I put it into work. I put it into nineteen-hour days, into pursuing impossible certifications, into being the most prepared person in every room. I told myself I was driven. I was. Just not in the way I claimed.

There is a particular pathology that comes from guilt-fueled excellence. Every project becomes existential. Every failure is not a setback, it is a verdict on whether your father's ruined hands were spent well. Other engineers go home at six. You don't, because you are not just doing engineering; you are arguing with the universe about whether you deserved the chance to do engineering at all.

This worked, professionally. It also made me a difficult person to be married to, a sometimes absent parent, and a man who never entirely believed his own success was real.

Dr. Cross, the mentor I described briefly in the earlier book without saying what made him unusual, saw it before I did. We were sitting in his office in late 1989. He had read a project I had stayed up four nights to finish. He looked at it, then he looked at me, and he said:

"Husam, you work like someone who has something to prove. You proved it. The question is when you start working for what you actually want to build instead of for what you think you owe."

I didn't have an answer. I went home and didn't sleep, again. He had named the engine.

What finally cracked it open was something my father said much later, in 1998, on a slow walk in Amman. I had moved closer to home, taken a less prestigious assignment specifically so I could be near him as his health worsened. I thought I was finally paying down the debt. We were walking past a grocery he used to send me to as a child. He was using a cane by then.

"You think too much about things that are finished," he said, quietly. "The accident taught you to be careful. The carefulness made you successful. Maybe it was meant to happen."

I wanted to argue. The "meant to" framing felt cheap to me, the kind of thing people say when they're trying to spiritualize damage. I started to push back. He held up the hand that didn't work properly anymore. He looked tired, but not the way I was tired. He had finished with this conversation a long time ago. I was the one who hadn't.

"Habibi," he said, "I forgave you long ago. The debt you are paying, I never wrote that bill."

I cried in a way I hadn't cried in years. Not because I was forgiven; I had always been forgiven. I cried because for the first time I understood that the debt I had been working off didn't exist outside my own head. My father had moved on. I was still paying installments.

I would like to tell you that the engine stopped that afternoon. It didn't. The compulsion to over-deliver is still in me. I still find myself working on projects with the intensity of someone repaying something. The difference is that I now know what I am doing while I do it, and sometimes, not always, I can choose to stop. That is not nothing. That is what change looks like in a person my age. Not transformation. Awareness.

I tell this story now because guilt-fueled excellence is one of the most common engines I have ever encountered, and one of the least examined. People build entire careers on debts they were never actually billed for. They overdeliver, overprepare, overwork, and they call it ambition because the word ambition is more flattering than the word penance. If you recognize yourself in any of this, the work is not to stop driving. The drive is real and it has built real things. The work is to find out, honestly, whose bill you are paying; and to ask whether the person who issued the bill ever actually sent it.

❖ ❖ ❖

Chapter 3

Lines I couldn't cross

I was five when I refused to eat meat for the first time. The story of the goat is in *Beyond Success*, so I won't retell it. What I will tell you is what the goat cost me four decades later in conference rooms.

A child who draws a moral line at five draws a moral line at fifty-five. The line moves around, the goat becomes a contract, the contract becomes a person, but the reflex is the same one. Something in me notices when the math is wrong, and the noticing isn't a choice.

This sounds noble in a memoir. In actual professional life, it is mostly inconvenient.

In a corporate meeting in 2014, I watched a colleague present a deployment plan that I knew, from technical work I had done two weeks earlier, would put a population of low-income users at risk for fraud. The risk was real but speculative; the deployment was real and revenue-generating. A reasonable person could have gone along with it. I was supposed to be the reasonable person. I was the senior technical voice in the room.

I raised the issue. I was told it was being managed. I asked specifically how. I was told the risk was acceptable. I asked acceptable to whom. The room got quiet in the way rooms get quiet when the thing being said is impolite, not because it is wrong but because it has stopped pretending the thing isn't happening.

I did not stop the deployment. I did delay it. I was, as a result, gradually moved off similar projects. Nobody fired me. Nobody yelled at me. Things just stopped flowing in my direction. I learned, again, that the cost of refusing to eat the meat is not that someone punishes you. The cost is that the family quietly stops making meals you can attend.

My mother, for a decade, prepared a separate plate for me at every dinner. Without complaint. Without making me feel like a problem. She also made sure I noticed she was doing it, in the only way she knew how, which was by leaving the small extra dish in the same place every evening, like a quiet flag. *I love you. This costs me. I am still doing it.*

I think about that dish more than I think about any management book I have ever read. It is the truest description of integrity I have. Not the line you draw. The price the people around you quietly pay because you drew it.

In professional environments, the people around you don't always pay quietly. Sometimes they pay loudly and resentfully. Sometimes they pay by routing around you. Sometimes they pay by promoting someone else. I have lost momentum I will never get back because of meetings I refused to be silent in. I do not claim this is heroic. I claim that it is the only way I knew how to keep recognizing the man in the mirror.

There was a stretch in the mid-2000s where I considered, seriously, whether the math had stopped working. Whether I should learn to swallow what other people swallowed. Whether the ethical reflex from the goat was a luxury I had inherited from a household where my mother could afford to make a separate plate. Maybe in adulthood the price was just too high. Maybe the goat was a children's story.

What pulled me back was realizing that I didn't actually have a choice. The reflex wasn't ideological. It was structural. I had been wired this way by a five-year-old refusing dinner, and the wiring was not optional firmware. I could either be the man my upbringing had built or I could try to be someone else and be miserable about it. I picked the first. It has cost me. I would pick it again.

The corporate world is full of people who can eat the meat. They run a lot of things. I am not them. There is a place for those of us who can't, even if it is sometimes a smaller place than we expected.

❖ ❖ ❖

PART TWO: WHAT SUCCESS COSTS

❖ ❖ ❖

Chapter 4

Foreign soil

I went to America at seventeen. I came back at thirty-eight. In between, I learned to perform being almost American.

The performance worked. I got the degrees. I got awards and recognition. I got the job offers and the title on the door. What the performance didn't do, what twenty-one years of careful assimilation didn't do, was make me feel like I lived where I was living.

In *Beyond Success* I described the early difficult parts: the supermarket cashier joking about how much bread we bought, the assumption that English-as-a-second-language meant intelligence-as-a-second-rate-capability. Those are stories that resolve. The cashier eventually moved on. The professors eventually saw the test scores. You assimilate. You succeed. The book ends.

The book ending is not when life ends. Life is what happens to you for the next thirty years after assimilation works.

Here is what worked too well: the skill of concealment. The refugee child who learned not to give people anything they could use against him grew into the executive who didn't quite know how to give people anything at all. I could perform warmth in a meeting and feel nothing. I could share a personal anecdote at a corporate dinner and have rehearsed it the night before. The competence of my self-presentation outpaced my self-knowledge for years.

The cost of this isn't visible from outside. From outside, it looks like polish. A quiet, capable man, easy in a room of strangers, never a wrong word. From inside, it is an exhausting low-grade translation that never stops. Every interaction is a cleaning operation: scrub the accent, soften the directness, file down the edges that mark you. By the end of a workday I would be tired in a way that had nothing to do with the work.

The harder part, the part I want my daughter to know about, is that this kind of competence prevents the connections that would actually fix what is making you tired. Real friendship requires that you let people see the unedited version. I had spent so long editing the version that I no longer remembered what the unedited one looked like. When colleagues invited me into their lives, barbecues, weddings, the small generosities that make a place feel like home, I performed gratefully and went home alone. They had no idea I was alone. I was their charming Husam. I had built him myself.

I want to be careful here, because I know how this sounds. I had a wife. I had children. I was not literally without people. What I was without was the experience of being seen as I actually was rather than as I had constructed myself.

The first time I was seen, really seen, was much later, by Tamara, when she was sixteen and asked the question that started this book. She had not bought the construction. She had grown up inside it and could see the seams.

I am still recovering from the discovery that the construction was unnecessary in most of the rooms where I deployed it. People weren't asking me to perform. I was performing because I had learned that if I didn't, in some other room, in some other decade, in a country I no longer lived in, I might not survive. The performance had outlived the danger by forty years and I had kept paying the rent on it because I did not know how to evict it.

This isn't a story with a clean ending. I am sixty-five and I still catch myself rehearsing. The difference now is that I notice. Sometimes I let the rehearsal go and let the actual sentence come out, and the sentence is slightly less elegant than the rehearsed one would have been, and the person I'm talking to looks slightly more interested rather than slightly less. That is the data point I keep collecting. People want the unedited version more than I trained myself to believe. The training was based on a country and a decade I no longer live in.

I am moving slowly. At my age you don't transform, you renovate, and you do it one room at a time.

❖ ❖ ❖

Chapter 5

When the founder died

The white envelope is in Beyond Success. December 2018. *Organizational realignment.* The corporate vocabulary for telling you that a business you helped build is no longer interested in keeping you in it. What that account did not include was the man who had built the place, and what his absence had let in.

The founder, I will not use his name; he was a friend, and I want to protect what was good about him, had been the kind of leader you do not find often. He shared credit. He took blame. He gave you room to do your work and then he stayed out of the way. We disagreed about plenty of things. We never disagreed about how to disagree. That was the rare part.

He died suddenly, in the autumn of 2017. One of those medical events that doesn't give you time to say goodbye. His twenty-four-year-old son inherited the business.

The son was not his father. This is not a moral indictment of him; he was twenty-four. He had not built the company. He had not earned the loyalty of the people who had. What he wanted, understandably, was a team that was loyal to him rather than to the memory of the man whose chair he had inherited. People like me, who carried that memory in our daily decisions, were inconvenient. The cleanest way to remove inconvenience is reorganization. Reorganization is a euphemism that means *you specifically but written so that it isn't actionable.*

The envelope wasn't a surprise by the time it arrived. I had felt it coming for three months. What surprised me was the grief.

I had expected anger. I had prepared for it the way I prepare for everything, methodically, with options, with savings. What I hadn't prepared for was how much of myself I had quietly given to a company that had just decided I was an acceptable loss. The years I would not get back. The relationships built on the assumption of long-term collaboration. The institutional memory that no longer had an institution to live in.

I cleaned out my office on a Friday. I had been there long enough to have a lot to clean out. I remember a photo on my wall, me and the founder at a Saudi Gazette event, both of us laughing about something that I now cannot remember. I sat with that photo for a long time and then I put it in a box and I left.

What I want to say about that period, the part I left out of *Beyond Success* because the wound was too fresh, is how quickly the people who had been your colleagues recategorize you. Not all of them. Some of them were generous. But enough of them shifted into a careful neutrality that I had to learn, all at once, what corporate friendship actually was. It wasn't friendship. It was professional adjacency that resembled friendship under the right conditions, and the conditions had changed.

The thing I keep returning to, looking back, is not the hurt. The hurt was real, but the hurt was also predictable. What I keep returning to is how much of my identity I had quietly outsourced to a job I did not actually own. I had been operating for years on the assumption that the institution would remember me because I had served it well. The institution did not have a memory. It had an org chart, and the org chart had been redrawn.

This was the first major lesson of the year that followed. Loyalty is a personal virtue. Companies are not capable of it. I had known this intellectually for decades. My body learns things slower than my head does, but once it learns them they stay learned.

The second lesson came a few weeks later, when a man named Damien, that is not his real name either, invited me to lunch.

I will tell that story in the next chapter. It is the part of my life I have most avoided writing about, because writing about it requires admitting how badly I, a man with three decades of experience reading people, misread one.

✦ ✦ ✦

Chapter 6

The predator

Damien is in Beyond Success. The events are there: the pitch, the missing titles, the slide that was mine and became his. What that account didn't tell you was why I walked in. This chapter is about the part of me that needed Damien to exist.

I had met genuine power before. I had briefed five-star generals about network security. I had advised members of royal families on technology strategy. I had sat in rooms with people whose net worth exceeded the GDP of several countries. The thing about those people, in my experience, was that they almost never performed power. They didn't need to. The room already knew.

Damien needed the room to know. He needed it loudly. His handshake lasted a beat too long. His eye contact was a competition rather than a connection. He used my first name twice in the first thirty seconds, the way a salesman does. I noticed all of this. I should have trusted what I noticed. I didn't, because Damien arrived three weeks after I left the blockchain company, and I was bleeding.

That is the sentence Beyond Success could not contain. *I was bleeding.* I did not walk into his company with my eyes open. I walked in still grieving the founder. Damien praised what I had built. He told me my expertise was exactly what his team needed. He used the phrase *complete autonomy.* It hit me in a place that was still raw from being told my experience was no longer required. It hit me in the place that had spent forty years trying to be sufficient.

I said yes for reasons I would not let myself examine until much later. The signing bonus was good. The title was good. The office was nice. None of those were the reason. The reason was that someone with a corner office had said *we need you,* and the part of me that had been a refugee child was still tracking, after sixty years, for any sign that I would be allowed to stay in the room.

The takeover happened in three stages, all of them recounted in Beyond Success, and I will not retell them here. The slide was the slide. The meetings became his meetings. By month six I was, quietly and politely, invisible inside a job he had hired me to lead.

What I want to record here is the technique. It is more common than you may realize, and I have watched colleagues fall to it twice since.

He gaslit by agreeing. *Yes, exactly,* he would say, when I made a point. Then he would describe the opposite of my point and tell me we were aligned. The first few times this happened I went back to my office and checked my own notes to confirm I had said what I thought I had said. I had. He had agreed and then said the opposite and called the opposite our shared position. The technique works on smart people because smart people extend good faith by default. Good faith is the vulnerability he was harvesting. If you are reading this and you are now thinking of someone you work with, trust the recognition.

The breaking moment came at a presentation to the executive team. I had spent six weeks building the analysis. The deck was scheduled under his name. I was listed as technical support. I sat in the back and watched him deliver my work as his insight, and when the executives asked technical questions, he paused thoughtfully and invited Husam to provide the detailed perspective.

I provided the detailed perspective. I did it cleanly, the way I would have done it if I had been the one giving the talk. I went home that night and sat at my kitchen table for two hours without eating. My wife brought me tea and did not ask. She knew what kind of quiet it was.

I drafted my resignation that night. I waited four days to send it, because I have learned not to send important emails inside my first emotional reaction. By the fourth day I was calmer and the letter said the same thing it had said on day one.

Within three weeks I had three offers from organizations that had heard, through whatever underground channels these things travel, that I had left. None of them mentioned Damien. All of them, in the interview, asked me what I had been doing for the last seven months, in the careful tone people use when they already know the answer. My value in the marketplace had not depended on his recognition of it. It had been there the whole time. He had spent six months constructing a story in which I could not generate value without his guidance, and the marketplace had quietly disregarded the story because the marketplace had access to my work history.

I will not tell you I left wisely or gracefully. I left exhausted. I left having lost the better part of a year to a man who was, in retrospect, transparently dangerous from the first handshake. I had ignored what I noticed because I needed the validation he was offering. The price of needing the validation was that I had to also accept the framework that came with it, and the framework was that I was raw material for his career.

The lesson I took from this was not about Damien. He is a known type. He will continue to exist because the corporate world rewards a confident lie more reliably than it rewards a humble truth. The lesson was about me. About what I was hungry for, and how that hunger had blinded me. After the founder's death, after the white envelope, I had needed someone to tell me my expertise still mattered. Damien had told me. I had not stopped to ask whether the person telling me was the kind of person whose endorsement I should accept.

You can be sixty years old, three decades into a successful career, and still get caught by this. That is the part nobody tells you. The patterns from childhood do not get smarter as you get older. They get more sophisticated about how they fail you. The refugee boy who was grateful for any kindness can still, at sixty, walk into a beautifully decorated trap, because the trap was baited with the exact phrase his five-year-old self had been waiting to hear.

What I do differently now is that I notice the handshake. When somebody holds it a beat too long and uses my name twice in the first thirty seconds, I do not ignore the data. I file it. I keep moving, politely, and I file it. So far, the filing has been correct every single time.

The other thing I do differently is that I let the kitchen table count as much as the boardroom did. It is where the actual work of the last decade has been done.

❖ ❖ ❖

PART THREE: WHAT I DO WITH THE REST OF IT

* * *

Chapter 7

The mirror

Farhan sent me a thank-you email three years after he left my team.

He had been a junior engineer when I hired him. I had spent two years coaching him, through technical challenges, through presentation skills, through the unspoken cultural code of an industry where his accent and last name marked him as an outsider, the way mine had marked me thirty years earlier. He had grown enormously. He had taken a strong leadership role at his next company. The email was warm and specific. He thanked me for things I had genuinely helped him with.

I read it. I felt something I did not expect.

I did not feel pride. I felt a kind of vertigo, as if a floor I had been standing on had shifted half an inch. The letter was real. The gratitude was real. What was unsettling was a question that arrived alongside it, uninvited: *had I actually helped him, or had I been working out something of my own through him?*

When I had taught him to project confidence in meetings, was that for his benefit, or was I reliving my younger self's struggle to be heard in rooms where my accent marked me? When I had pushed him to claim credit publicly, was that good mentorship, or was it my own decades-old wound about Damien doing the work for me twenty years too late? When he succeeded, did I feel proud of him, or did I feel relieved about something in me?

The answer, I think, is both. Mentorship is rarely clean. The people who tell you it is clean, are usually selling something.

I had walked into mentorship, decades ago, with the conviction that I would do it differently than the predators I had met. I would share credit. I would push my mentees forward instead of stepping in front of them. I would use my position to elevate them. All of this is true, and all of this is what I did. None of it is incompatible with the parallel reality, which is that I also chose mentees whose struggles resembled my own and whose victories functioned, secretly, as redemptions for the parts of me that hadn't yet healed.

This is not a confession of bad faith. It is a recognition that the same wound that drove me to be useful to younger engineers also shaped which engineers I noticed and what I thought their problems were. I was probably an excellent mentor for the people who reminded me of my younger self. I have to wonder how I did with the people who did not.

Aisha was the one who made this concrete for me. She had been a mentee for two years, not the loudest member of the team, not the obvious choice for the high-visibility projects. I had helped her transition from engineering to product management. She wrote me a note after she landed her dream job. The note said something that, on a first read, was a compliment:

Thank you for helping me figure out my own path instead of trying to make me follow yours.

It was a compliment. It was also a diagnosis. She was telling me, kindly, that what had been useful about our work together was the thing I had done less of than I usually did. I had projected less of my journey onto hers. She had needed less management than the version of me from ten years earlier would have provided. I had, almost by accident, given her something better than my expertise: I had given her room.

I am still figuring this out. I think the mentor I would now want to be is the one who does very little. Asks the right questions. Stays out of the way of someone else's discovery. I am not naturally that person. I am naturally a fixer, show me a broken thing and I will reach for the cloth before you finish the sentence. My sister Samia said it to me once, during a foundation meeting, in the tone she uses when she's about to take me apart with affection.

Abu Amer, she said, using the family nickname, *you are still that boy in the courtyard wrapping cloth around the chick's broken leg.*

I had forgotten the chick. Samia hadn't. She has carried a fifty-year inventory of my reflexes, the way an older sister will, and she had named the one I most needed to be aware of. The reflex is good. It has shaped my whole life. It is also the reflex that, undirected, can cause you to wrap a person who didn't ask to be wrapped, and to call it help.

The hardest part of mentorship is not the giving. It is the discipline of giving only what was asked for, which often turns out to be a lot less than what you wanted to give. People have to walk their own road. Even when you can see the potholes from where you are standing. *Especially* when you can see the potholes, because seeing the potholes is what convinces you that you should walk the road for them, which is the temptation you most have to refuse.

Farhan's email is still in a folder in my inbox. I reread it sometimes. It is a good letter. He is a good engineer. I helped him. I was also, while helping him, helping a younger version of myself. Both of those things are true. The trick of integrity is being able to hold them in the same hand without flinching.

❖ ❖ ❖

Chapter 8

What Tamara saw

The summer Tamara turned seventeen, she came home from a refugee camp outside Amman and she was different.

She had spent eight weeks volunteering with Syrian children. She had been doing service work since she was twelve, that is part of what her mother and I had tried to give her, but this was the first time the service had been with people whose experience overlapped with her father's. She had grown up hearing stories about Amman. She had not, until this summer, walked through a camp like the ones my parents had passed through after 1948.

She came back with a clarity I recognized but had stopped feeling.

"Dad," she said one night at dinner, "some of these kids don't have a single toy. They play with empty bottles. I asked one of them what he did for his birthday. He looked at me like he didn't understand the question."

I could imagine what she was describing, in the technical sense, I had lived a less acute version of it. What I noticed about her statement was that I had, somewhere in the previous twenty years, stopped imagining it. I had moved my own childhood into the past tense. It had become content for keynotes. It was no longer a present reality demanding a present response.

"Why don't we do more?" she asked.

I had a list of answers. We donate. We support educational initiatives. We give back. The answers were true. They were also, every one of them, an accommodation of the gap between what we were doing and what was possible. Tamara was not asking whether we were doing enough relative to other people in our income bracket. She was asking whether we were doing enough relative to the need.

I tried, briefly, to give her my answer. I watched her face. She was not unkind. She was just unconvinced. The arguments I had constructed over twenty years collapsed inside ten seconds because she had not been raised inside them and had no investment in keeping them upright.

A few weeks later she announced she wanted to start a foundation. Not for basic needs, there were already organizations doing basic needs. For *joy*. For birthday parties for refugee children. For the celebration of a child's existence as something worth celebrating, regardless of whether that child had a passport or a permanent address.

I want to be honest about my first reaction. My first reaction was to soften it. I started thinking about scope, about sustainability, about the pitfalls of well-intentioned amateur philanthropy. All of these are real concerns. They were also, I see this now, my way of moving the conversation from her territory back to mine. She was operating on moral simplicity. I was offering operational complexity. Operational complexity is one of the senior tools that men of my generation use to neutralize the moral simplicity of younger people.

Tamara did not let me. She had absorbed my management style well enough to recognize when it was being deployed against her. She listened to my caveats, nodded, and then said:

"Okay, so help me build it correctly."

I did. We co-founded the Smiles Foundation. She named it. She runs the program design. I do the operations and the boring legal infrastructure that keeps the doors open. We have served thousands of children. We will serve thousands more. The foundation is the most meaningful thing I have built in fifteen years and almost none of the strategic vision was mine. It was hers.

What she gave me, what I had not realized I needed, was the experience of building something whose center of gravity was outside my own healing. The foundation is not me processing my refugee childhood through service. It is, mostly, my daughter responding to a need she encountered, and me being useful to her response. The shift in those prepositions matters. *Through me* versus *for her* turns out to be a different kind of work entirely.

I will tell you the unsentimental thing. The work is not always joyful. Children need lots of things and we cannot give them all of those things. There are families we cannot reach. There are administrative rooms that exhaust me. There are weeks I want to write a check and walk away. What keeps me in the room is watching my daughter at work. She is a more efficient moral agent than I have ever been. She does not carry the freight I carry. She just sees what is needed, figures out who can do it, and does it. She is what an adult who was not formed by war looks like.

I did not give her that. Her mother and I tried very hard to make sure she did not need to be formed by what formed me. The success of that intention is its own paradox: the daughter who does not understand my hypervigilance, who walks into rooms without looking for exits, is the daughter who is teaching me how to be useful without using my service to repair myself.

There is a particular kind of grace in being out-mentored by your child. I don't recommend resisting it. The first time I tried to resist it, I lost the argument inside thirty seconds. By the second time, I had stopped trying.

◆　◆　◆

Chapter 9

What the institutions taught me

A note before I close the book.

I have spent my career inside or adjacent to institutions that present themselves as forces for good. Universities. Multinational corporations. Governments. International bodies whose acronyms I will not list. I am not going to write the cynic's chapter that pretends I figured out, late in life, that all of this is a sham. It isn't. There is real work being done by real people inside these places, and a lot of that work is good.

What I will say is that institutions do not have consciences. They have processes. The processes can be steered, briefly, by people with consciences, but the steering does not survive the person. Whatever you build inside an institution, the institution will continue without you, and it will continue without remembering why you built what you built.

This sounds obvious in print. It is not obvious in practice. I spent most of my forties believing that if I could just get the right policy adopted, the right system implemented, the right governance structure approved, the institution would carry the value forward. It does not. The institution carries the artifact forward. The value evaporates with the people who held it.

I helped build technical systems that I am proud of. Some of those systems have, in the years since I built them, been deployed against the very populations they were meant to serve. This is the deepest grief in my professional life. It is also the experience that has most shaped how I now think about the relationship between technical work and political reality. Knowledge without conscience becomes a weapon. The conscience has to be carried by individual human beings, every day, inside the institution, by name, with consequences. There is no algorithm for this. There is no policy. There is only people, choosing, repeatedly, whether to be the one who says the inconvenient sentence in the meeting.

I have watched democratic societies, including the one I lived in for twenty-one years, become more outraged about delayed flights than about systematic oppression. I have watched colleagues whose work I respected disappear, professionally, after raising concerns about how their tools were being used. I have watched, in the last decade, the moral floor of professional life lower by inches that nobody acknowledged in real time but that, looking back, summed to a meter.

I am not telling you this to despair. I am telling you because I am old enough now to know that the institutions will not save themselves and that you do not have to single-handedly save them in order to keep doing useful work. What you have to do is preserve the small space inside yourself where you still notice the math being wrong, and refuse to let the noticing be retired by reasonableness.

I am still inside institutions. What I have learned about being an insider is that the most useful thing I can do is preserve the ability to look at any given decision and ask, plainly: *who does this actually serve?* That question gets harder to ask the higher you go. The price of asking it gets bigger. The number of people who will tolerate hearing it gets smaller.

I keep asking it. I lose some battles. I win some. I stay on speaking terms with most of the people I disagree with. I do not pretend this is sufficient. It is what is available to me. It is what is available to anyone, at any level. The work of conscience inside institutions is small and daily and mostly unrewarded, and as far as I can tell it is the only work that ever actually moves anything.

◈ ◈ ◈

Chapter 10

The Next Chapter

Tamara is in her twenties. She runs her Smiles Foundation without me in any meaningful sense; my role is mostly to stay out of the meetings she runs better than I would. She has also founded a startup called Gaia, focused on women's health, an industry I know nothing about but she appointed me as her co-founder and CTO. She is outspoken. The people she works with respect her.

She has called herself, more than once and not as a joke, an enhanced version of me.

I want to be careful with how that landed. It was not a boast. It was the kind of observation a young person makes when she has grown up close enough to a parent to know the engineering of him, and she is reporting back, not on his deficiencies, but on what she has done with the schematic. *Enhanced version*. The phrase has stayed with me. There is something in it I am still learning to receive without flinching.

Because it is also true.

She has the parts of me that I would have wanted to give her. The intelligence. The relentlessness. The moral reflex I described earlier, the one that draws a line at five years old and keeps drawing it. She has it. The reflex is sharper in her than in me, because she did not have to file it down to survive in rooms where people misheard her name.

She also has the parts of me I tried to spare her. She is slim, the way I was slim. She eats slowly, with the same selectiveness that, when she was younger, gave her mother a version of the difficulty my mother had with me. Different food, different decade, same shape. A mother accommodating a child whose appetite is a kind of statement. I had not expected that pattern to repeat. We had been so careful. Children are not inputs to a system, no matter how carefully the parents try to engineer the inputs.

She can be alone. She is comfortable in her own company in a way that is both a gift and a thing I recognize from a long way away. I have written in this book about the cost of the hypervigilance, the inability to relax, the performance that outlived the danger. Tamara does not have my hypervigilance. She does have my self-sufficiency. She does not need other people the way most twenty-one-year-olds need them. This is one of the things she got from me that I am not fully sure I should have given her. Self-sufficiency keeps you upright. It also keeps people at a distance you do not always want.

So she is not the daughter who is unmarked by what marked me. She is the daughter who is differently marked. She has her own version of my armor, lighter, better fitted, less visible to the people who meet her. The question I sit with now is whether the lighter armor will ask less of her than the heavier version asked of me.

I think it will. I have to think it will, because I am out of time to test the alternative.

The work she is doing is not a continuation of mine. The Smiles Foundation began as her response to refugee children she saw on TV in the comfort of her safe home, not as my second act. Children who spent cold winter nights in tents. Gaia is a women's health company, in a domain I am not equipped to navigate and have, on her instruction, stopped trying to. She is doing her own work, with her own framework, in her own century. What she got from me, and from her mother, and from my parents, and from the grandparents she knows only from photographs, she has metabolized into something that is neither replication nor reaction. It is hers.

This is what I think I have been trying to say, in my whole career, about education and capability and the democracy of intelligence. The point was never to clone myself forward. The point was to ensure that whatever was useful in what we had been given, mostly through suffering we did not choose, became raw material for something better in the next generation. Tamara is what better looks like, this round.

When I was thirty I thought the goal of a life was to finish something. Finish the company. Finish the patent. Finish the proof that the refugee boy had become an engineer and his father had not lost his fingers for nothing. I did not finish any of that. I built things, and the things had their seasons, and the seasons ended, and I was always still walking.

What I have come to understand, watching her take the moral architecture I gave her and renovate it for purposes I do not fully understand, is that there is no finishing. There is only handing forward. The things I built will not outlast the institutions that house them. Tamara will. Her work will. Whatever she chooses to give the people who come after her will. The currency that survives is the kind my mother bet on when she taught us that knowledge could not be confiscated. The currency was never the patent. It was the daughter.

I am not the protagonist anymore. I am the previous chapter. The next chapter sometimes quotes from this one in passing, occasionally ironically. This is, as far as I can tell, the correct order of things.

She is the chapter now. Whatever I had to say in this book about the body keeping score, about the goat I refused to eat, about Damien, about the institutions without memories, about waking before dawn for forty years, was the long preface to the sentence I am writing now. The sentence is short.

She is the chapter.

My job is to step back far enough to let her have the room. I am working on the stepping back. The reflex to fix is fifty years deep, and the work of not fixing is the work I am doing in the early-morning hour I used to spend rehearsing things I did not need to rehearse.

Some days I succeed. Some days I do not. The fact that I notice the difference now is what I am calling progress, at sixty-five. It is not nothing.

She will not need this book. She is already past most of what is in it. But the people who read it, the ones who recognize themselves in the early-morning hours, who built something and then wondered who they built it for, who left a country and never quite arrived in the next one, may need to know how the story ends.

It ends with my daughter. It ends with me getting out of her way.

◆ ◆ ◆

Integration

There is a question I am not going to answer in this book, which is whether I am healed.

I am not. I will not be. At sixty-five, healing is no longer the right word for what I am doing. I am integrating. The wars are inside me and they are not leaving. The lawnmower is inside me. Damien is inside me, smaller every year, but inside me. The founder's funeral is inside me. Jim's funeral is inside me. So is my mother's saj. So is my father's last walk in Amman. So is my daughter, sixteen, asking me a question I could not answer.

I carry all of this. So do you. So does everyone past a certain age. The question for the second half of life is not whether you can put it down. You can't. The question is whether you can carry it without it hardening into bitterness.

What I have come to think, provisionally, with the caveat that I might be wrong, and that anyone who writes a memoir at sixty-five with confident conclusions has not been paying attention, is that the difference between bitterness and wisdom is whether you let your wounds talk to you or whether they talk *for* you.

A bitter man's wounds do the talking. He has stopped arriving at sentences from the present. Every sentence comes from 1966, or 1972, or 2017. You cannot have a real conversation with him because he is not in the conversation. He is in the wound, looking out.

A wiser man, and I do not claim to have arrived; I claim to be walking, keeps his wounds informed but not in charge. The wound contributes data. It does not write the policy. The wound knows what dangerous looks like. It does not get to declare every situation dangerous.

The work of staying out of bitterness is daily. It is small. Some mornings I lose. I wake up at 4 a.m. and the wound is in charge for an hour before I can pry the steering wheel back. By six I am usually myself again. By eight I am dressed and useful. The hour between four and five is the war. It will be the war for the rest of my life.

I am not asking for sympathy about this. I am telling you about it because I think most people my age are running similar wars and not telling anyone, and the not-telling is the part that hurts more than the war itself. If you are forty-five and reading this and the early-morning hour is yours too, you are not unwell. You are doing the work that nobody warned you the second half of life would consist of. The work is real. The fact that it does not show up on your résumé does not mean it is not happening.

I want to leave you with three small things, because lists of three are the cliché I have been refusing for ten chapters and at this point I have earned one.

First: nothing in your life that mattered came from the parts of you that were polished. It came from the parts that were broken and that you used anyway. The polish is for the photographs. The work is done by the rest of you.

Second: the people who tell you success will fix you are selling you something. Success will not fix you. It will rearrange the room in which the unfixed parts of you have to live. That is a real improvement. It is not the same thing as fixing.

Third: the job is to be useful while broken. Not to be perfect. Not to be finished. Not to be inspirational. Just to be useful, today, in a way that is still recognizable as you. That is enough. It has had to be enough for me, and it has, on most days, turned out to be.

I am going to put down the pen now. The boy who walked ten kilometers to school is still walking. The hour before dawn is starting to get light. There is work today, and there will be work tomorrow, and at some point, not soon, I hope, but at some point, there will be a Tuesday that turns out to be the last one.

Until then, this is what I have to offer. The road, and the willingness to keep walking it.

That, in the end, is what I think *unbroken* means. Not undamaged. Not unhurt. Not whole.

Still walking.

— Husam

❖ ❖ ❖

About the Author

Husam Yaghi was born to a family displaced in 1948. A Palestinian-Jordanian engineer with a Ph.D. in computer science and a degree in electrical engineering, he has spent more than forty years in technology: building companies, publishing research, and advising governments and royal families on technology strategy.

He is a husband and a father. He supported his daughter in building the Smiles Foundation, which brings birthday celebrations and small joys to refugee children. He supports his wife in her charity work. He continues to wake up before dawn and writes even if nobody reads.

Beyond Success told the story of what was built.

Unbroken tells the rest.